out of the
shadows
and into the
world

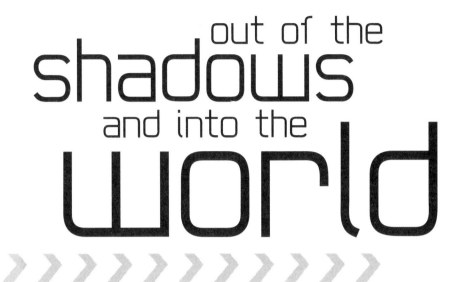

out of the
shadows
and into the
world

>>>>>>>>>>>>>>

scott dawson & jay strack

THOMAS NELSON
Since 1798

NASHVILLE   DALLAS   MEXICO CITY   RIO DE JANEIRO

© 2011 by Jay Strack

All rights reserved. No portion of this book may be reproduced, stored in a retrieval system, or transmitted in any form or by any means—electronic, mechanical, photocopy, recording, scanning, or other—except for brief quotations in critical reviews or articles, without the prior written permission of the publisher.

Published in Nashville, Tennessee, by Thomas Nelson. Thomas Nelson is a trademark of Thomas Nelson, Inc.

Thomas Nelson, Inc. titles may be purchased in bulk for educational, business, fund-raising, or sales promotional use. For information, please e-mail *SpecialMarkets@ThomasNelson.com*.

Unless otherwise indicated, Scripture quotations are taken from THE NEW KING JAMES VERSION. © 1982 by Thomas Nelson, Inc. Used by permission. All rights reserved.

Quotations noted The Voice are taken from The Voice™ Bible. © 2012 Ecclesia Bible Society. Used by permission. All rights reserved.

Scripture quotations marked NCV are taken from the New Century Version®. © 2005 by Thomas Nelson, Inc. Used by permission. All rights reserved.

Portions of this guide marked "Adapted from the Impact Bible" have been adapted from the Impact Student Leadership Bible by Jay Strack (Thomas Nelson, 2008).

ISBN 978-1-4016-7524-0

Printed in the United States of America

11 12 13 14 15 PP 5 4 3 2 1

contents

Introduction 7

Lesson 1: Out of the Shadows (Luke 24) 11

Lesson 2: Into the World (Acts 1 and 2) 25

Lesson 3: Ministry at the Gate (Acts 3 and 4) 37

Lesson 4: The Prize Is Worth the Commitment (Acts 6 and 7) 51

Lesson 5: Blinded by the Son (Acts 9). 67

Lesson 6: Kidnapped by Angels (Acts 12) 77

Lesson 7: They Turned the World Upside Down (Acts 17). 91

Lesson 8: Emerge and Engage (Acts 26) 109

introduction

» OUT OF THE SHADOWS AND INTO THE WORLD STUDY GUIDE

This study comes within the context of your life journey. It's a journey that begins the moment you were conceived, and it will continue throughout your existence. There are certain things your soul longs for on this journey and, whether you've realized it or not, your life is shaped by your search for them—worth, significance, acceptance, love, peace, and beauty are needs felt by all.

Nearly everyone has a burning desire to discover a reason for their existence. We feel an all-consuming need at our very core to discover meaning and purpose in life. Our search may take us down many roads. Wherever our life choices take us, we all continually seek the way to have our deepest needs met.

The need to know our purpose and the persistent yearning to have our soul's genuine needs met was placed within us by our Creator God. He wants us to seek for the only thing that will ever truly satisfy our souls— the Person of Jesus Christ.

Only through Him will we ultimately discover our soul's contentment. Our souls cannot discover rest, until we rest in Him.

We are a people wired to worship. We can't help that. All of us treasure something or someone above anything else in our lives. We give our devotion to somebody or something. So the question isn't "do we worship," the question is "what are we worshiping."

Each person knows the inner hunger to find real answers to the very genuine questions we all share. As we walk together through these few sessions, we will begin to discover truths about our world and about ourselves. We can support and encourage each other along the way as we travel together on this journey toward understanding our search for identity and meaning.

» OUT OF THE SHADOWS AND INTO THE WORLD GROUP EXPERIENCE

Our search for meaning in life can be a lonely quest. We make wrong turns and often end up lost. By joining together with others as you pursue the truth behind your desire to find meaning and significance, you join with fellow travelers who are trying to navigate the same road. By using this study guide within a group you can offer encouragement to one another which cannot be overrated.

While walking this road together, you'll encounter real-life situations and emotions that will challenge you; and by exploring and sharing your hopes, dreams, insights, successes, and failures with one another you will grow in your journey with Christ.

In order to create an environment where each person is free to be authentic and open, it's important to agree on some small group ground rules from the start. First, create a "safe zone" for your group. This means that nothing said in the group can be repeated outside the group. Each person's story is his or her own and should only be told by that person. Treating one another with respect and compassion will create a true sense of community which will grow from session to session. In this environment of respect, you should value and protect each other's emotional, spiritual, and physical space; no one should devalue a fellow group member in any way, and no one can be touched by another person without permission.

The purpose of your small group is to invite open and honest sharing from your life, but there are some circumstances that call for limited sharing. Steer clear of sharing anything that will put another person in jeopardy, could lead to legal problems, could reflect poorly on someone else, or that you don't have clearance or prior permission to speak about.

Everyone should feel free to share without receiving criticism, advice, or condemnation. You will be on a journey of discovery, telling your own stories and encouraging others to do the same. When someone shares, be sure to thank them for sharing or ask a follow-up question to clarify something they said. Sharing is not an invitation for lecture, correction, or judgment. Your group should be a safe place for all—a place where each person is encouraged to participate as they are able. Avoid letting one person dominate the conversation. Instead, operate according to 1 Corinthians 13:4–7, giving to each other true love, kindness, and patience; bearing, believing, hoping, and enduring all things.

So as we agree to be real with ourselves, each other, and God, let's begin. Let's help one another come to the place where we can all learn to say "No" to the things that have held us back in the past and "Yes" to God's purpose for our lives.

» HOW TO USE THIS GUIDE IN A GROUP

If you are using this guide in a group, your group may not always get through all of the questions in each session. That is just fine. There may be certain questions that hit home with your particular group and will take up the majority of time for that session. The point is not to get through all the questions. Just use these questions as a way to dig deep into each life within your group. It might help to record any extra notes or thoughts you may have in conjunction with this guide.

out of the shadows
Luke 24

» PURPOSE

In the very last chapter of his gospel, Luke wants us to know that God came into history through the Person of Jesus Christ, in order that we might see and investigate the God who performs the supernatural as He reaches out to His creation.

» BACKSTORY

Luke wants us to know that in order to save the world Jesus chose not to save Himself from the pain and suffering of the cross. Jesus lived the only perfect life, impacting us two thousand years later. He invested His life into His twelve disciples and other followers by teaching, equipping, and mentoring them. Luke ends his gospel with an account of those who were eyewitnesses to the miracles of Christ. They hid behind locked doors,

A.D. 30	A.D. 33	A.D. 59–60
|	|	|
Public ministry of Christ begins	Crucifixion Resurrection 3 days later	Book of Luke written

burdened with fear, doubts, and uncertainties after the world turned on Jesus. As they remembered the words of Christ, these believers emerged from the shadows and found confidence. (Adapted from the Impact Bible)

"This ending point becomes the starting point for Luke's sequel, known as the Acts of the Apostles. The story isn't really over; it's just begun. The life and ministry of Jesus that Luke has just recounted is the mustard-seed stage of the kingdom of God that continues to grow and grow and grow. Now it's time for this Kingdom to fill the world. If Luke's gospel is about what Jesus began to do and teach, then Luke's sequel is about what the risen Jesus continues to do and teach through His followers for millennia." (The Voice, page 1285)

》 CHARACTERS

Luke: The author of the Book of Luke; a physician and a co-worker with Paul. An educated man who interviewed those who were eyewitnesses of the life and works of Christ, then wrote their stories for the generations to come. He was not one of the original disciples.

Mary Magdalene: Healed by Jesus of seven demons.

Mary, the mother of James and wife of Clopas: Possibly a relative of Mary, the mother of Jesus.

Joanna: The wife of Chuza, Herod's finance minister.

The Disciples: Eleven of the twelve men who traveled with Jesus and were eyewitnesses to His power. They personally saw the miracles and were discipled by Jesus' words.

Jesus: The resurrected Christ; He appears three times in this chapter.

Angels: Messengers of God sent to the women to announce the Resurrection.

» THINK: PUT YOURSELF IN THE STORY!

Early in the morning, Mary Magdalene, Joanna, and Mary of Clopas went to the tomb, but they found the stone rolled away and the tomb empty. Two angels came and told them, *"He is not here, but is risen! Remember how He spoke to you when He was still in Galilee, saying, 'The Son of Man must be delivered into the hands of sinful men, and be crucified, and the third day rise again.' And they remembered His words"* (Luke 24:6–8).

The women took this message to the disciples, who were hiding in the shadows behind closed, locked doors, and then Peter ran to see it for himself. He saw the empty tomb, but doubt and uncertainty ruled him, even though Peter had seen the miracles and power of Christ firsthand.

Two of the early followers traveled to a nearby town called Emmaus, and as they walked, Jesus appeared, but they did not recognize Him. Jesus asked the men why they were sad, and one answered, "Are you the only person in Jerusalem who doesn't know that the chief rulers delivered Jesus, a prophet mighty in deed and word, to crucifixion? We thought He was the one who would save Israel. Now His body is missing and they say He is alive." Jesus patiently began to teach them, again, all that the prophets wrote in the Scriptures concerning Himself. They asked Him to stay for dinner, and as He blessed the bread, their eyes were opened and they knew Him.

Immediately, they returned to Jerusalem, found the other disciples, and told them, *"The Lord is risen indeed!"* (Luke 24:34). As they were telling them this news, Jesus appeared out of nowhere and said, *"Peace to you"* (v. 36). Instead of rejoicing, the disciples were afraid, and Jesus

EMERGE|N|ENGAGE

The disciples were living in shadows, terrified for their lives and uncertain of what the future held. Jesus commanded them to engage the world. Only the Word of God was able to calm their fears and bring the truth to the forefront. It was what they *already knew*—the words of Jesus—that ultimately gave them power to emerge into the world.

There is a pattern here: Jesus led the disciples to EMERGE from shadows of doubt, fear, confusion, and uncertainty by REMEMBERING the Word of God.

13

asked, *"Why do doubts arise in your hearts?"* (v. 38). He showed them His hands and feet, and then reminded them again: *"Thus it is written, and thus it was necessary for the Christ to suffer and to rise from the dead the third day, and that repentance and remission of sins should be preached in His name to all nations, beginning at Jerusalem. And you are witnesses of these things"* (vv. 46–48).

》 DREAM: JUST IMAGINE IF . . .

1. The disciples focused on His death (the negative shadow), not on the words that promised His resurrection (the positive emergence). What they saw—*His death*—became more powerful in their minds than the truth they knew—*His resurrection*. Is there something you "see" (for example, insecurity, rejection, family pressure, gossip, loneliness) that is stronger in your mind than the truth you already know?

What sin habits do you see that are so rampant they seem normal even though you know they are not?

Give an example of something in media or music that teaches a different view of sexual intimacy than what the Word of God does. How is it made to look normal or mainstream?

Read the instruction in 1 Peter 5:8 to be sober-minded. How would you compare this command with culture's much more casual attitude toward drug and alcohol use?

sober: to have a sound and healthy mind; to guard with a wall; to watch, and be mindful.

In other words, *pay attention to what you allow into your mind.* When a person uses alcohol and other drugs, he or she opens the gate to problems such as depression, anxiety, oppositional defiant disorder, and antisocial personality disorder. This is the total opposite of emerging from shadows and emerging with positive leadership into the world!

2. Describe a time when you felt confused or scared. It could involve a family situation, peer pressure, health issue, money problem, friendship, or anything else.

With that in mind, is there any biblical principle or Bible verse you *remember* that would change how you feel about your confusion and fear? What is it? Write it here as you remember it.

FLIPSIDE

Think of a situation where you made the wrong choice. What verse or Scripture might have helped you to think differently?

3. Have you heard that women were not valued in biblical times? Maybe you have even been told that women are devalued in today's churches?

Read Luke 24:1 and 10. Who was first told of the Resurrection?

Why do you think were they were the first ones Jesus entrusted with the news?

What do you think this shows about Jesus' attitude toward women and His level of respect for them?

DO-OVER

What is one choice you have already made that you wish you could do over?

Are do-overs necessary because people *forget* or because they *ignore* God's Word? Explain.

» LEAD: EARN THE RIGHT

1. In Luke 24:25 Jesus called the disciples *slow of heart*. What do you think this means? How does it affect leadership?

In this digital age, with Scripture readily available on your phone, tablet, or computer, why is it still important to memorize Scripture?

King David, a man after God's own heart, said this: *"Your word I have hidden in my heart, that I might not sin against You"* (Psalm 119:11). You cannot remember what you don't know!

2. In Luke 24:31–33 distraught disciples making their way back home to Emmaus had an experience with the resurrected Christ. They *emerged* from the shadows of sadness and guilt and *engaged* with other believers to encourage them. The *slow of heart* became filled with excitement and *[their] heart[s] burned within [them]* (v. 32). Why? What happened?

How long has it been since your heart "burned within" as the Spirit revealed the Son through His Word? Too long? Pause now and ask the Lord to meet you in His Word, bringing revelation and life. Ask Him to join you often and open the Scriptures to you, making them come alive by His Spirit. (Adapted from the Impact Bible)

3. Notice that the disciples' past experiences, even though they were eyewitnesses to Christ's power, were not enough to empower them with boldness or confidence. Jesus had to remind them and teach them, once again, the Word of God. Why do you think people tend to "save up" or rely on their spiritual experiences from various events rather than find power in God's Word daily? Has this happened to you?

Does checking in with God once a week at church give you enough power to live a godly life all week long? Why or why not?

Think again about the difference between *having access* to Scripture and *knowing* Scripture.

Scripture is like a river, broad and deep, shallow enough here for the lamb to go wading, but deep enough there for the elephant to swim."

Gregory the Great [A.D. 540–604] *Moralia in Iob, Book 1.*

4. Luke 24:18–21 reveals that the disciples' desire to stay in the shadows was caused by hoping in something Jesus never promised them. He never said He would redeem Israel, at least not in the way the disciples thought; He told them He would be crucified for the sins of the world. They wanted revenge against the Romans; He came to give victory in their own personal lives. They wanted a *better* life; He came to give *new* life.

Leaders may long for an easier life, one in which standing for truth is not so difficult; but Christ died, rose again, and filled us with His Spirit to give us the strength to walk in the midst of difficulty with confidence in His Word and bring others along with us.

>> The circumstances of life don't change; *we do!*

>> A leader's first thought and first action step is positive.

>> He or she is willing to do the hard thing.

EMERGE | N | ENGAGE

Compare Luke 24:7 with Luke 24:46, 47. What does it mean that *repentance and remission of sins should be preached in His name to all nations* (v. 47)? How would you compare that directive to someone saying to you, "Get out of the huddle and into the game!"?

Why does verse 7 say Jesus *must* be crucified?

repent: turn around in your behavior; go the other direction

- Give God the opportunity to blot out your sin (Acts 3:19).

- Allow the goodness of God to lead you to repentance (Romans 2:4).

- *Godly sorrow produces repentance leading to salvation, not to be regretted.* (2 Corinthians 7:10).

How would you explain that to a friend who doesn't understand Christianity or is having a hard time believing?

Where does your "Jerusalem" begin (v. 47)?

DID YOU KNOW ?

>> There are twenty major religions in the world; thousands of sects of those religions; millions of pagan gods and idols.

>> There is only ONE who resurrected Himself from the dead!

>> REMEMBER

Then He said to them, "Thus it is written and thus it was necessary for the Christ to suffer and to rise from the dead on the third day."

—Luke 24:46

into the
world
Acts 1 and 2

» PURPOSE

If we do the possible, God will do the impossible. Jesus told the disciples to *"go into all the world and preach the gospel to every creature"* (Mark 16:15), but first He said, "Wait in Jerusalem for the gift my Father has promised" (Acts 1:4). Going out to all the world was not physically or financially possible for the disciples at the time, so we see in Acts 1 and 2 that God brought the world to them.

» BACKSTORY

The Bible is filled with miracles. Three of those miracles, the greatest events of history—the resurrection of Christ from the dead; His bodily ascension into heaven; and the fulfillment of the promise on the Day of Pentecost—changed the world forever. God brought people from every

A.D. 33	A.D. 33–59	A.D. 60–61
Birthday of first church	Acts of apostles	Book of Acts written

nation in the world that day to witness a miracle that only He could perform so that He could go home with them as they spread the good news around the globe.

It might seem silly to some to believe in miracles. After all, we have technology and science that can invent and reveal an ever-expanding amount of knowledge, and most things can be "explained." Remember that only God can *create;* the rest of us work with what He has already made.

Some liberal biblical scholars have attempted to dismiss the reality of miracles by explaining them away with science. But what they and we need to remember is that the evidence should form our conclusions, instead of our conclusions shaping the evidence. Without the basic foundational element of God's existence, one will always search for a naturalistic answer that can explain away the miracles. The birth, life, death, and resurrection of Christ form the greatest evidence for the miraculous. God came into history through the Person of Jesus Christ in order that we might see and investigate the God who does the supernatural. (Adapted from the Impact Bible)

》 CHARACTERS

Theophilus: His identity is a mystery. He might have been either a new convert in need of discipleship or an interested Greek whom Luke hoped to convert through his researched life of Jesus in the Gospel of Luke and now further evidence of His resurrection power in the Book of Acts.

The risen Christ: Jesus, the crucified Christ, has risen from the dead.

Disciples: Peter, James, John, Andrew, Philip, Thomas, Bartholomew, Matthew, James, Simon the Zealot, Judas the son of James, Matthias (who replaced Judas).

Mary, the mother of Jesus: Jesus' mother, who was often present with Him throughout His ministry; here she is with the disciples awaiting His next instruction.

Brothers: The half-brothers of Jesus; they thought He was crazy while He was on the earth, but after the Resurrection, they came to believe.

Prophet Joel: Minor prophet of the Old Testament, he wrote the Book of Joel, which teaches of the "day of the Lord" approaching and the importance of repentance.

Luke: The author of the Book of Acts, a physician and eyewitness to the missionary thrust of the early church.

» THINK: PUT YOURSELF IN THE STORY!

Jesus had told His followers to wait for the promise of the Father at Jerusalem. And yet, even as Jesus stood before them in His resurrected body—the miracle of all miracles—they continued to ask Him when He would restore the kingdom of Israel! He answered, *"It is not for you to know times or seasons which the Father has put in His own authority. But you shall receive power when the Holy Spirit has come upon you; and you shall be witnesses to Me in Jerusalem, and in all Judea and Samaria, and to the end of the earth"* (Acts 1:7–8).

After He said this, the disciples literally watched Him be physically, bodily taken up to heaven in a cloud. Two men, probably angels, stood by and said, *"This same Jesus, who was taken up from you into heaven, will so come in like manner as you saw Him go"* (Acts 1:11).

Obviously stunned, but also encouraged, the disciples went to an upper room of a house and stayed there praying and praising. They

feast of pentecost:

One of the three holy feasts of the Jews, celebrated at the temple, a one day festival celebrated at the end of the barley harvest. This was a joyous time of giving great thanks to God.

day of pentecost:

The birthday of the church, when the Lord kept His promise and poured out His Spirit.

organized their leadership, choosing to replace Judas with Matthias (Matthew).

When the great Day of Pentecost came, they were all with one purpose and in one place and suddenly there came a sound of rushing mighty wind that filled the whole house. The disciples were all filled with the Holy Spirit and began to speak in other tongues. Hearing the commotion, a crowd gathered, and the people from every nation under heaven heard preaching in the language of their country and even the dialect of their particular region. They were amazed and said, "How is it that we are hearing our own language spoken by men who do not know our language?" Some were excited, but others said the disciples were just drunk.

The apostle Peter stood up and said, *"[We] are not drunk . . . But this is what was spoken by the prophet Joel: . . . 'I will pour out My Spirit in those days, and they shall prophesy. I will show wonders in heaven above and signs in the earth beneath. . . . And it shall come to pass that whoever calls on the name of the LORD shall be saved'"* (Acts 2:15, 16, 18, 19, 21).

Peter went on to expound about Jesus being rejected and crucified, and raising victoriously from the grave. When the crowd heard this, they were *cut to the heart* over their actions and asked, *"What shall we do?"* (Acts 2:37).

Peter answered, *"Repent . . . be baptized in the name of Jesus Christ for the remission of sins"* (Acts 2:38). He continued on preaching truth, and about three thousand people *gladly received his word* (v. 41). All who believed were joined in a common purpose and sold their possessions and goods to give to those in need.

Every day they *continued steadfastly in the apostles' doctrine and fellowship . . . and in prayers*, staying united in purpose, and eating together from house to house with gladness, praising God, and having favor with all the people (Acts 2:42). *And the Lord added to the church daily those who were being saved* (v. 47).

» DREAM: JUST IMAGINE IF . . .

1. Throughout the Book of Acts, we see that people respond one of three ways before receiving Christ:

   » *apathy*: the absence of emotion, as in "I don't care"

   » *curiosity*: an interest or desire to know or understand

   » *hostility*: unfriendly opposition

   Which of these was Paul's (Saul's) response? (Refer to Acts 9.)

   Which of these was the response of the brothers of Jesus? (Refer to Mark 3:20, 21; John 7:5.)

ascension:

Jesus made many appearances after His resurrection over a period of forty days. He then was taken up into heaven from the Mount of Olives with a promise He would return in the same manner (Acts 1:9–11).

What about the disciple Thomas? (John 20:24, 25)

Remember Zacchaeus? How did he respond? (Luke 19:1–6)

Can you think of any others in the Scripture who responded in one of these three ways?

What about people you know who were prayed for and finally turned to Christ? What was their initial response?

Is there someone you could put on your prayer list who needs to move out of apathy, curiosity, or hostility? Write their name below. Believe God can do it today!

FLIPSIDE

The ascension of Jesus and the Day of Pentecost changed the world. What if the Holy Spirit had never come? Imagine …

2. The New Testament church is about a cooperative spirit. A portrait of the early life of the church provides characteristics of community:

》 There was unity of mind and heart because individuals were led by the Holy Spirit.

》 The atmosphere was one of humility and servant leadership.

》 There was great power when proclaiming the gospel of Christ.

》 There was an intense emphasis on the responsibility that all physical needs be met.

(Adapted from the Impact Bible)

Read Acts 2:42–47. Pick out five words or phrases that directly resulted in *the Lord add[ing] to the church daily those who were being saved* (v. 47).

The message of God is that although Jesus' *earthly* work is finished, He sent the Holy Spirit to work through us as we carry on the mission through servant leadership.

EMERGE N ENGAGE

Jesus ascended to heaven to take His rightful place at the right hand of the Father. He had to leave so that the Spirit of Truth, the Promise, could come.

》 LEAD: EARN THE RIGHT

1. Most people think of the Holy Spirit as being essentially about power, but that is only one aspect of Him. We must also understand the Person of the Spirit to truly know and experience God. The Holy Spirit is a Person with a distinct personality. Get to know Him by looking up these verses:

He speaks	Acts 13:2
He prays for us and with us	Romans 8:26
He forbids us and leads us	Acts 16:6, 7
He guides us to truth	John 16:13
He convicts us of sin	John 16:8
He may be resisted	Acts 7:51
grieved (as in, to make sorrow)	Ephesians 4:30
quenched (to put fire out)	1 Thessalonians 5:19

The Holy Spirit is powerful; He is coequal to God, coeternal and coexistent. Both the Old and New Testaments identify Him as God.

He is called God explicitly	Acts 5:3, 4;
	1 Corinthians 3:16;
	2 Corinthians 3:17
His power is unlimited	Luke 1:35
He is omniscient	1 Corinthians 2:10

Look up the word *omniscient* and write the meaning here:

_____

He is omnipresent   Psalm 139:7–10

Look up the word *omnipresent* and write the meaning here:

_____

He is everlasting   Hebrews 9:14
He was part of creation   Genesis 1:1, 2
He is called the Helper   John 14:16, 17
                                                   (Adapted from the Impact Bible)

2. Servant leaders are Holy Spirit-filled leaders. Based on what you have learned about the Person of the Holy Spirit, what types of qualities should a leader or influencer seek to possess?

3. Servant leaders are Holy Spirit-filled leaders; their influence is timeless and boundless (to the end of the earth; ever expanding). Acts 1:8 says, *"But you shall receive power when the Holy Spirit has come upon you; and you shall be witnesses to Me in Jerusalem, and in all Judea and Samaria, and to the end of the earth."* How can a person who might live seventy or eighty years have timeless and boundless influence?

4. *"You shall be witnesses to Me . . ."* What are you bearing witness to?

Love comes from God and God is love	1 John 4:7, 8
God is caringly involved with our ways	Psalm 139:3
God longs to show us grace and compassion	Isaiah 30:18
God in Christ has made provision for sin	Romans 3:23; 6:23
His abundant life is ours for the asking	John 10:10
Whoever calls on His name shall be saved	Romans 10:13

(Adapted from the Impact Bible)

Have you ever wondered how you would lead someone to a personal faith in Christ? Look at the above list and think about these words: *believe, trust, accept, repent, call . . .*

Using those words (*believe, trust, accept, repent, call*), can you write a three to five sentence prayer of salvation that you can lead a person in who wants to receive Christ as Savior?

» REMEMBER

*"But you shall receive power when
the Holy Spirit has come upon you;
and you shall be witnesses to Me in
Jerusalem, and in all Judea and Samaria,
and to the end of the earth."*

—Acts 1:8

ministry
at the gate
Acts 3 and 4

≫ PURPOSE

Acts 3 and 4 show us the result of the Day of Pentecost in Acts 1 and 2. We see that being filled with the Holy Spirit results in bold proclamation of the gospel of Christ and a unified church.

≫ BACKSTORY

It became clear that Christianity was growing rapidly among the people, including thousands of Jews. These Christians acknowledged that Jesus was the one true Messiah, and the priests were nervous about this. The Roman Empire ruled Israel at this time, and the Jewish priests stayed close to the rulers in order to get what they wanted. In this case they wanted to stop Peter and John from spreading the good news of Christ. The priests didn't care if that meant killing them, imprisoning them, or just intimidating them through persecution. But the priests mistakenly thought

A.D. 33	A.D. 33–59	A.D. 60–61
Birthday of first church	Acts of apostles	Book of Acts written

it was by Peter's and John's own power that people were responding to the gospel; they did not understand that it was the Spirit of God who was working in the hearts of the people. They tried to bring the apostles to a trial, just as they had done to Jesus, but the Lord intervened.

The bold apostles publicly held all the house of Israel responsible for the death of Jesus and consistently preached the Resurrection. After the miracle of Pentecost, Peter and John marched boldly forward, and there was a special spirit of unity and purpose among the new Christians. God blessed their attitudes and their hearts and the church continued to multiply across the lands. (Adapted from the Impact Bible)

» CHARACTERS

Peter: A fisherman, he was called by Christ to be one of the twelve disciples. He loyally followed Jesus throughout His earthly ministry, then betrayed Him three times on the night of His crucifixion. Jesus appeared personally to Peter and forgave him, after which Peter courageously preached the gospel and wrote 1 and 2 Peter of the New Testament.

John: One of the original disciples, called John the Beloved, he is the one Jesus turned to on the cross to care for His mother, Mary. He wrote the Gospel of John, the epistles of John, and the Book of Revelation.

Beggar: A man who had never walked since birth and was carried by various people to the gates of the temple to beg for money.

Priest of the Jews: One who made sacrifices, performed rituals, and acted as a mediator between man and God in the temple of Jerusalem.

Sadducees: A Jewish sect who did not believe in the resurrection. They followed only the law of Moses.

» THINK: PUT YOURSELF IN THE STORY!

Peter and John went to the temple at prayer time and saw a lame beggar who lay helpless every day at the Gate Beautiful. Being moved to compassion, Peter said, *"Look at us,"* and the man did because he thought they were going to give him money (Acts 3:4). *"Silver and gold I do not have,"* Peter said, *"but what I do have I give you: In the name of Jesus Christ of Nazareth, rise up and walk"* (v. 6). He lifted the man up and immediately he was strong and jumped up onto his feet. The beggar began to dance and praise God, and he walked into the temple beside Peter and John. The people crowded to see him because they knew he was born crippled and had never walked in his life!

Peter asked the people why they were marveling at this, since he did not do it of his own power, but Christ's. Then he began to preach of repentance of sin and of the death and resurrection of Jesus.

The priests, captain of the temple, and the Sadducees were upset that Peter and John preached of Jesus' resurrection from the dead. They grabbed them and put them in jail, but some five thousand who heard them teach of Jesus believed that day!

The next day Peter and John were brought before the leaders of the high priests. The leaders asked them, *"By what power or by what name have you done this [healing]?"* (Acts 4:7).

Peter, filled with the Holy Spirit, said, "Are you judging us because of a good deed to a helpless man? You should know it was by the name of Jesus Christ of Nazareth, the very one you

the gate beautiful:

Eight gates surrounded the temple of Jerusalem. It was a magnificent building with large porches and many elevations of courts around it—one of the wonders of the world. People flocked to the temple, some just out of curiosity, others to sell sacrificial animals or exchange money, some to gossip and people watch, and some to give praise to God in worship. The Gate Beautiful was completely covered with gold and silver, which prompted Peter's statement to the beggar, *"Silver and gold I do not have..."*

39

herod's temple: This was

the second temple of the
Jews: the first was built
by Solomon, and this
one was rebuilt on the
same site by Herod. The
entrance plaza was the
size of twenty football
fields. Josephus the great
historian wrote that it
"caused an amazement
to the spectators, by
reason of the grandeur
of the whole....and
took ... over forty-six
years to build."

crucified and who has risen from the dead, that he stands here well!"

"Nor is there salvation in any other, for there is no other name under heaven given among men by which we must be saved" (Acts 4:12).

The priests saw that Peter and John were uneducated and untrained but very bold, and they were stunned. Realizing these men had actually been with Jesus while He was alive, they didn't know what to do. They couldn't deny the power of what happened, but could not commend it either for fear that people would start to believe. So they resorted to the only thing they could come up with—threatening Peter and John with beatings and jail if they continued to speak and teach in the name of Jesus—and then let them go.

Peter and John ignored the threats of the Sadducees, and as soon as they were released, they went straight to their friends, told them what happened, and everyone praised God with one voice and said, *"Lord, You are God, who made heaven and earth and the sea, and all that is in them. . . . Now, Lord, look on their threats, and grant to Your servants that with all boldness they may speak Your word"* (Acts 4:24, 29). They continued on praying in the name of Jesus, and suddenly the place was shaken and they spoke the Word of God boldly through the Holy Spirit.

Instead of the movement of God being stopped, it grew faster. Not only did more people believe, they also became compassionate and caring and worked confidently with one purpose. Even some of those who were once enemies started to believe, and the fearful became courageous. All who owned lands or houses sold them and brought them to the apostles to distribute to anyone who had a need. Because of this act of selfless giving, the witness to the resurrection of the Lord Jesus went out with great power.

》 DREAM: JUST IMAGINE IF . . .

1. Peter said, *"In the name of Jesus . . . rise up and walk."* Name some ways you can become engaged in a hurting person's life (for example, mission trips, prayer, donating time, money or aid, or raising funds within a group).

EMERGE|N|ENGAGE

The pressure to stay quiet is not new. We face it often. The city leaders tried to intimidate Peter and John, but they boldly emerged from the shadows.

The power of AND:

We might see the need, but walk by without engaging.

Christ calls us to both see the need AND meet the need.

FLIPSIDE

If you cannot say, "Rise and walk in the name of Jesus," what can you say to someone who is hurting?

But what about personally? *The Power of And*: Name a need you have seen. How you can engage to meet it on a personal level?

How important was it that Peter and John took the healed beggar *into* the temple *with* them?

From a testimony standpoint?

From a fellowship standpoint?

Inviting is different than taking someone with you; picking up, giving a ride is different than "See you there if you can make it"; handing out a tract or information is different than engaging through listening and meeting a need.

2. Peter said, *"Look at us."* He wanted the man to look him in the eye. What does this say about Peter's level of engagement?

When you see a beggar or homeless person, what do you do as you walk by?

DO-OVER

Have you ever snubbed someone without meaning to as you walked by? Try this out on a friend: compare what happens when you just walk by and nod versus stopping to look them in the eye and speak. That's the power of AND. Talk for a minute about eye contact and its impact on your communication to others.

In addition to wanting to look him in the eye, what might be another reason Peter wanted the lame man to look away from the silver and gold gates?

Doesn't it happen to all of us? We focus our eyes and hopes on material things, on what the world calls valuable. Can you think of anything we might focus on that takes us away from looking to Jesus?

3. Matthew 26:69–74 tells us that just a few weeks earlier Peter denied Jesus THREE times. Now he has emerged from the shadows and stands boldly to speak, even though he is in danger of persecution. What happened to change Peter's heart between the betrayal and the boldness?

4. Look at Acts 4:1–4. Some five thousand people were saved that day! How important was Peter's decision to stop and engage with *one* man? Did that one healing have much to do with what happened?

Look through the passage and explain how all the events worked together to end with such an amazing result.

If you can't feed a hundred
people, then just feed one."

Mother Teresa

» LEAD: EARN THE RIGHT

1. Look at Acts 4:1–12. The Sadducees did not believe in the
resurrection and tried to have Peter imprisoned. Yet he immediately
answered them by preaching that Jesus died and was risen from the
dead! Truth is truth, and there is no denying it—even if someone
else doesn't believe it.

Leaders take the risk when they know they stand for truth.
Never be ashamed to emerge from the crowd and stand for the cause
of Christ. If we are not standing now, we will not be able to in that
moment either. What would you do if you faced persecution for
speaking about Christ?

List two moral values that you would be willing to stand up for in
public (for example, abstinence, the right to defend the Bible publicly,
prayer in schools).

2. In Acts 4:29 the disciples prayed for boldness to speak God's Word. What does it mean to be bold? Does it imply arrogance, defiance, or confidence?

How does a person become confident in their faith?

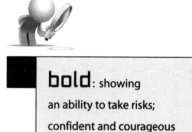

bold: showing an ability to take risks; confident and courageous

Can you give an example of a bold statement about the Word of God?

3. Look at Acts 4:31. Some people say that to be *filled with the Spirit* you have to get more of God, but others say He has to get more of you. Which one is correct and why?

What was the result of the disciples being filled with the Holy Spirit?

4. Refer to Acts 4:13. What is the driving force in a leader that gives him or her the boldness to publicly defend their faith?

Is this available to everyone or just a chosen few?

How does a person become a leader for Christ?

What might prevent you from being filled with the Holy Spirit of God?

How do you want people to describe you? Fun, popular, cool?

Wouldn't you like to be described this way: *They had been with Jesus!*

》 REMEMBER

> *And when they had prayed, the place*
> *where they were assembled together*
> *was shaken; and they were all filled*
> *with the Holy Spirit, and they spoke*
> *the word of God with boldness.*
>
> —Acts 4:31

the prize is worth the commitment
Acts 6 and 7

》 PURPOSE

Acts 6 and 7 show us that influence is the result of serving and private victories precede public victories. Stephen, an important person in these chapters, shows us how to stand against criticism and error. In him we see the first martyr and the reality of heaven. The death of Stephen forced the church out of its comfort zone; they became the witnesses Jesus called them to be, taking His Word throughout the regions of Judea and Samaria.

》 BACKSTORY

Stephen was chosen as a servant leader and became the first Christian martyr. Although we think of a martyr as someone who died for the faith, the Greek word for martyr means "a witness," and it referred to someone

A.D. 33	A.D. 33–59	A.D. 60–61
I	I	I
Birthday of first church	Acts of apostles	Book of Acts written

who gave testimony through words and actions to things they had experienced. The early believers did not—indeed they could not—get over the radical transformation they experienced through the gospel. Many early believers were killed because of their unwavering commitment to Christ, leading to the use of "martyr" to describe such faithful witnesses.

For many early Christians, it was better to die than to stop testifying about Christ. They were also known as proclaimers, as in those who declare publicly and shamelessly. It was with this type of fervor and passion that early church leaders devoted themselves. Whether they lived or died, the goal was to preach Christ and His resurrection. (Adapted from the Impact Bible)

》 CHARACTERS

Stephen: A man of good reputation because of his faith and godliness. He was the first martyr of the Christian church.

Synagogue of the Freedmen: A Greek-speaking Jewish synagogue, perhaps made up of descendants of Pompey's prisoners of war in 63 B.C.

Sanhedrin: The ancient Jewish court system; the supremely religious in the land of Israel.

Saul: A Pharisee intent on persecuting Christians and stopping the gospel, he later was transformed by Christ and became Paul, the apostle.

》 THINK: PUT YOURSELF IN THE STORY!

Suddenly the growth of the church was exploding! As the news about the resurrected Jesus spread, the disciples saw that more servant leaders were needed to minister to the less fortunate. The resumé of those chosen had to read: *good reputation, full of the Holy Spirit and wisdom* (Acts 6:3).

One of those chosen was Stephen, a man full of faith and the power of the Holy Spirit and who *did great wonders and signs among the people* (Acts

6:8). The Synagogue of Freedmen began to oppose him, but they could not stand up to his wisdom, since the Holy Spirit was guiding Stephen's words.

Since they could not find any way to argue what Stephen was saying, they decided to secretly plot against him by making up lies. They presented the lies to the Sanhedrin council, but when they looked at Stephen they *saw his face as the face of angel* (Acts 6:15). So they asked him, *"Are these things so?"* (Acts 7:1). Stephen began to take them through Jewish history and the Scriptures; it was obvious he knew the Word of God well as he presented it from memory right on the spot.

They were listening intently as he expounded from Abraham and Moses to David and Solomon. Then Stephen looked at them and said, *"You stiff-necked . . . in heart and ears! You always resist the Holy Spirit. . . . you now have become the betrayers and murderers, who have received the law by the direction of angels and have not kept it"* (Acts 7:51, 52, 53). The accusation of killing the Messiah cut deep and made Stephen's listeners angry enough to want to kill him.

Stephen, *being full of the Holy Spirit, gazed into heaven and saw the glory of God, and Jesus standing at the right hand of God,* and he told the people what he saw (Acts 7:55). They started to scream and attacked him in one huge crowd, running Stephen out of the city where they could stone him to death. Even during this he was saying, *"Lord Jesus, receive my spirit"* (v. 59). Before he died, Stephen forgave his attackers, crying out, *"Lord, do not charge them with this sin"* (v. 60). And the witnesses laid down their clothes at the feet of a young man named Saul.

》 Stephen emerged as a leader because he was full of God's grace.

》 He courageously engaged in a debate against false doctrine and unbelief.

》 To engage in battle against false doctrine, we need the powerful combination of the grace of our Lord Jesus and the truth of the Scriptures.

》 DREAM: JUST IMAGINE IF . . .

1. Read Acts 7:17–53. The Voice Bible gives an interesting perspective on Stephen's address in these verses: "It is one thing for [Stephen's] audience to agree that idolatry was a problem in the past and another when they are charged with the accusation of the same idolatry in the present. According to Stephen, those who reject Jesus are following the same path as the people who rejected Moses to follow idols" (page 1338).

FLIPSIDE

As young leaders we must realize that we judge ourselves by our motives, but we judge others by their actions. Describe what modern-day idols you see and why you would define them as such.

2. Read about Stephen's opposers in Acts 6:9–15. Lies, criticism, and secrets. Sound familiar? Some things never change.

They argued with Stephen (v. 9)

They secretly met to gossip about him (v. 11)

They convinced others to be angry (v. 12)

They lied (v. 13)

How do you feel when someone tells lies about you?

idol: an object of worship

- a person, more important than your relationship with Christ

- pleasure, something you are not willing to give up or turn from

- a possession, something you want badly enough you will do anything to get it

When you are criticized, what is your first response?

If someone gets angry at you, do you usually yell or get angry in return?

DO-OVER

Think about a time when you were confronted with a lie, criticism, or anger. What do you wish you would have done differently in the situation?

Read about some responses to lies, criticism, and anger:

» Stephen had "The Glow that Shows": *And all who sat in the council, looking steadfastly at him, saw his face as the face of an angel* (Acts 6:15).

» Moses came down from meeting with God and his face glowed: *And whenever the children of Israel saw the face of Moses, that the skin of Moses' face shone . . .* (Exodus 34:35).

» Jesus went up into the Mount of Transfiguration to pray: *As He prayed, the appearance of His face was altered, and His robe became white and glistening* (Luke 9:29).

A reputation comes about by what one shows to others!

Character is when we keep promises we make to others." Integrity is when we keep the promises to God and to ourselves.

Student Leadership University syllabus

3. Stephen was given a chance to escape when the men asked him, "Are these things true?" He could have said anything and worked his way out of a dangerous spot, but he presented the Scriptures boldly from memory.

Think about being at a party, a club, or a classroom where your values are being challenged. You are thrown the ball: "What do you think?" Are you ready to answer? Do you *know* the Scriptures?

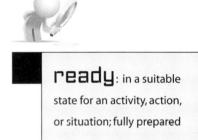

ready: in a suitable state for an activity, action, or situation; fully prepared

First Peter 3:15 says, *But sanctify the Lord God in your hearts, and always be ready to give a defense to everyone who asks you a reason for the hope that is in you, with meekness and fear.* How can a Christian be ready to give an answer?

What is one subject or belief you hold that you might be or have already been questioned about?

Name two things you can do this week to start getting *ready* (for example, research Acts characters online, talk to a Bible teacher, read a book about Paul, ask questions, focus reading in Luke 24 and Book of Acts):

1. _____

2. _____

4. In Acts 7:56 Stephen says, *"Look! I see the heavens opened and the Son of Man standing at the right hand of God!"* Jesus gave Stephen a standing "O." Imagine, the Savior of the world standing to receive one of His children into heaven.

   Acts 6:8 says Stephen was *full of faith and power*. How does a person become full of faith and power?

Do you think it was easier for Stephen to share the gospel in his day? Before you answer, remember he was walking in a land filled with pagan idols and false gods, in a time when religious leaders wanted blood to stop Christians.

We know that Stephen first saw Jesus in the Scriptures and through the everyday choices of his life before he saw Him in heaven. Is this what gave him the courage to continue?

What or who gives you the courage to follow God?

Stephen saw Jesus standing in heaven to receive him and it motivated him to finish well. In the end he decided the prize was worth the pain. What did Stephen do to cause Jesus to stand in his honor? Was it the final act of martyrdom or was it his everyday life?

» LEAD: EARN THE RIGHT

1. As the early church began to grow, the apostles realized they needed more servant leaders. They were looking for *men of good reputation, full of the Holy Spirit and wisdom* (Acts 6:3). Anyone who submitted a resumé for the job had to be able to display these qualities more than any abilities.

    Suppose tomorrow your church sends out a blog looking for servant leaders with a similar description. Can you apply?

How can you tell what a person's
reputation is?

reputation:

a widespread belief that
someone or something
has a particular habit or
characteristic

Does it really matter how we act and react to people or situations?

Stephen was described as *full of faith and power*, doing *great wonders
and signs among the people* (Acts 6:8). How can you know if a person
is full of the Holy Spirit?

What about full of wisdom?

2. As followers of Jesus we all have access to the *faith, power, and the Holy Spirit* that defined Stephen, but how we submit to these aspects makes the difference.

DISCUSS

Discuss the definitions of the terms below: *fan, follower, faithful*.

Jesus is Present: We are **fans**

fan: a person who has a strong interest in or admiration for a particular sport, art form, or famous person

Jesus is a Priority: We are **followers**

follower: devotee of a particular person, cause, or activity

Jesus is Preeminent: We are **faithful**

faithful: loyal, constant, and steadfast

These three ideas (fan, follower, faithful) are all good, but how would you rate them as to good, better, best?

Can a "fan" be a person who does not know Christ personally?

Can a "follower" be one who follows rules and teachings, but does not have a personal relationship?

Can a "faithful" person be anything but consistent?

3. At the end of Stephen's message the crowd was *cut to the heart*—in other words, he got to them (Acts 7:54). Their response was to stone him to death. Stoning involved throwing small stones so that many people could take part in delivering the punishment; in this way, no one person could be branded a murderer.

What "small stones" might you be throwing on a daily basis that might cause others to stumble in their faith or to be discouraged: things like gossiping, ignoring people, or acting one way around certain people and another way around others?

4. Notice what happened after the death of Stephen. The people laid down their clothing at the feet of a man named Saul (Acts 7:58). Saul later converted to Christianity and became the great apostle Paul, but for now and a long time afterward he was a hater of Christians, one who beat, imprisoned, and had them killed.

Read Acts 7:60. Do you think God might have used these last words of Stephen in the life of Paul later on?

Think of someone you know who is opposed to the teachings of Christ. Do you think anything you say or do can ever have an effect on their heart?

》 REMEMBER

But sanctify the Lord God in your hearts,
and always be ready to give a defense to
everyone who asks you a reason for the hope
that is in you, with meekness and fear.

—1 Peter 3:15

blinded
by the son
Acts 9

》 PURPOSE

Jesus interrupted Saul's malicious plans with one of His own. Saul, once a ferocious persecutor of Christians, was driven to his knees to proclaim Christ as Lord, and he never stopped doing so until the day of his death. His story is given to us in Acts 9 as an example of how telling your personal story can win men and women to Christ—the ultimate emergence from shadows into engagement with the world.

》 BACKSTORY

Saul was raised in Tarsus, a town known for its school of philosophy. He was educated by the great Pharisee teacher Gamaliel. In Tarsus Saul would have been influenced by Greek philosophy, Roman economics, and Jewish religion. He was no doubt a man of influence and culture with a pedigree for success. And though Judaism did not teach hate, Paul

A.D. 33	A.D. 33–59	A.D. 60–61
|	|	|
Birthday of first church	Acts of apostles	Book of Acts written

was zealous in his intention to persecute Christians. He was involved in the stoning of Stephen and he incited riots against the early believers. Probably hoping to guarantee his status with the Sanhedrin, Saul chased down Jesus-followers, which led him to Damascus.

» CHARACTERS

Saul: A Pharisee who persecuted Christians.

Ananias: A man of Damascus called by God to go and minister to Saul.

Jesus: The risen Christ personally intervened, blinding Saul and turning him to salvation.

» THINK: PUT YOURSELF IN THE STORY!

Saul was a madman on a mission of rage to destroy anyone who claimed that Christ was the Messiah. He was well educated and highly connected and wanted to use political pressure to legally threaten, persecute, and even murder anyone who was called a follower of "The Way." While on his way to Damascus, Paul was blinded by a great flash of light and fell to the ground. The thunderous voice of the Lord asked, "Saul, why are you attacking me?" Saul responded to the question with a question—"Who are you?"—but we can be pretty sure he already knew it was the Lord!

"I am Jesus," the voice replied, "the one you are attacking. Go enter the city and you will be told what to do next."

Paul's companions, frightened by his sudden blindness, led Saul by the hands to the city of Damascus, where he stayed three days without eating or drinking.

During that same time, the Lord visited a disciple named Ananias through a vision and told him, "Go to the street called Straight and ask about Saul of Tarsus. He is praying to Me at this moment and has had a vision of you coming to lay hands on him and restore his eyesight." When

Ananias heard the name "Saul of Tarsus," he questioned the Lord, saying, "We have all heard of this evil man who has come to imprison us."

"Yes," said the Lord, "but you must go so that I may show him all that he must endure and suffer for My name's sake."

So Ananias went as he was instructed, laid hands on Saul and called to him: *"Brother Saul, the Lord Jesus, who appeared to you on the road as you came, has sent me so that you may receive your sight and be filled with the Holy Spirit"* (Acts 9:17). Immediately, scales fell from Saul's eyes and he could see. He was baptized, and after spending time with the disciples in prayer and study, he began to preach about Jesus in the synagogues. Imagine how amazed the Jewish priests were! This same man sent letters ahead to say that he was coming to persecute and imprison Christians and now he was preaching Jesus as the Son of God! People were amazed, and Saul began to grow more confident in his call, debating anyone who would listen to him speak of the Son of God whose name is Jesus.

power: forceful strength; might. In the Greek, it is the word *dunamis*, the same word from which we get *dynamite*. The power of the gospel exploded in Paul's life; he then took the gospel around the world with confidence.

Do you have *dunamis*? How does a person become *confident* in their faith?

But those who heard him could think of nothing but what they had done to Jesus, and they tried to kill Saul. The disciples heard of the plot, put Saul in a basket at night and lowered him down over the city wall. The plan worked and he returned to Jerusalem where he continued his preaching ministry. And Saul, who became Paul, was used to change the entire world with the love of Christ, just the way he had been changed.

» DREAM: JUST IMAGINE IF . . .

1. Do you ever think someone has gone too far or done too much to come to Christ? Do you know someone you think is unreachable for Christ? It would have been easy to think of Saul this way. Read his biography in Philippians 3:4–7. What comes to mind as you read these verses?

Notice Paul's humility in verse 7: *But what things were gain to me, these I have counted loss for Christ.* The things that once were so valuable to him were no longer important. He EMERGED from the past. That's the sign of a new life!

2. Student Leadership University grads are answering the personal call of God on their lives to change the world: Here are just a few . . .

   » At age nineteen, Justin Miller began starting medical clinics in Kenya and now is up to fourteen working, successful clinics (www.careforaids.org).

   » Emily Buchanan became the youngest director of a national non-profit working to raise awareness for the rights of the unborn (www.sba-list.org/).

》 Caleb Clardy moved to New York City to plant a church in the heart of the city as his first full-time job (www.trinitygracechurch .com).

These began as ordinary teens with extraordinary passion and vision. If God does indeed use anyone who is willing, how many people can He use you to reach? Start making a list of people for whom you will pray, and to whom you will present your story.

2. When Paul met Jesus, he knew he had found the real thing. No longer was life about the law; it became about grace. If anyone would understand being forgiven, wouldn't it be Paul, the once persecutor and murderer of Christians? Anyone else might have gone into hiding, but instead Paul wrote in Romans 1:16: *For I am not ashamed of the gospel of Christ, for it is the power of God to salvation for everyone who believes, for the Jew first and also for the Greek.*

3. In Acts 9:8–9 Saul was suddenly blind for three days and had no idea why or what was to come next. Imagine how horrible that would be! He was literally led around by friends as he waited for Jesus to reveal the next step. He had no one to trust but Jesus. In those three days, something stirred deep within him and he was able a short time later to step into the synagogue and publicly declare, "Jesus is God's Son!"

Have you ever experienced a time when you or someone you love felt helpless and had no choice but to trust Jesus? What happened? How did that turn out?

Sometimes there are just too many options in life, and Jesus becomes our last choice. Not because we don't love Him, but because we allow noisier people or things to crowd Him out.

A few years ago, Tarra Dawson, the wife of evangelist Scott Dawson, came within hours of losing her sight. In her own words, it was like "looking through wax paper at a flashlight moving slowly away." When the doctor said there was nothing else he could do, she turned her attention to prayer and introspection.

Tarra will tell you that an intimacy began with her Lord like none she had ever experienced before. She was wholly dependent. You will never understand intimacy with Jesus until you are dependent upon Him.

It is a terrible thing to see and have no vision."

Helen Keller

» LEAD: EARN THE RIGHT

1. In Acts 9:10–16 Ananias was told to go to Straight Street and minister to Saul. He must have stared at that door a while before he had the courage to knock. He reminded the Lord that he had heard of this Saul—he had heard that Saul was evil. God essentially said, "I know, get going. I will take it from here."

2. Read Acts 9:22–27. It's not surprising the Christians didn't believe Saul and still feared him; the Jews hated him and wanted him dead. But a few disciples decided that helping Saul was more important than fear.

When the Jews plotted to kill Saul, the disciples let him down the city wall in a basket. Saul was the one called miraculously by God, the one the Lord would use to speak to thousands and to write the New Testament. But the ones who held the rope saved his life. Their act of faith became a part of Paul's ministry forever.

EMERGE | ENGAGE

The great thing about being faithful when God calls is that you will always be in the right place at the right time. Are you content to go through the motions of life or take a daring adventure with Christ? Ask Him for a "Straight Street" to travel down, a task bigger than yourself, something so outrageous that only God can do it.

FLIPSIDE

> How would history be different if the disciples hadn't taken the chance to help Paul escape?
>
> Servant leaders know they might not be called to preach or be out front in ministry, but they can hold the rope and be a vital part of ministry to this generation. Name some tasks in ministry that might be classified as "holding the rope."

3. Saul was transformed into Paul, the greatest missionary to the Gentile world. WOW! God always has a way of using the wrong person for right things. Pick two of your favorites below and read their Scripture story.

>> *Moses*: He was called to be the spokesperson, but told God he was slow of speech (Exodus 4:10).

>> *Abraham*: He was called to be the father of many nations while he was over ninety years old and childless (Genesis 15:1–7).

>> *David*: He was called to be king, even though he was the youngest of his brothers (1 Samuel 16:7).

>> *Peter*: He was so unstable, but Jesus called him Peter, which means "rock" (Matthew 16:18).

>> *Mary*: She was an unmarried teenage girl. God gave her the fate of all mankind (Luke 1:30–37).

>> *Saul*: He hated Gentiles but he was transformed to Paul, the missionary to the Gentile world (Acts 9).

When Scott Dawson was a freshman in high school, he had a speech impediment, weight issues, a lazy tongue, and thick glasses (every girl's dream!). Today Scott is an evangelist with a national ministry (www. scottdawson.org). He says, "It blows my mind to see how God can reach down and touch someone and transform them through the power of His Spirit and allow them to stand before people." You may think that God cannot use you, that God doesn't understand what you have gone through or experienced. You may even have thought you wanted to do something for God, but that you were the wrong person. But there is good news: God is waiting for us to realize we are the wrong person so He can do something right in our life.

 There is something called Instant Success, but nothing called Instant Maturity."

Adrian Rogers

4. Do you have a Damascus Road story? You may not have been blinded, but what was the day or time when God called you to salvation? Think about it for several minutes and replay that time in your mind. If you can't think of a time, if you are not confident in your personal salvation, don't be embarrassed or afraid, be excited!

There are people who would love to talk with you. Contact someone in the church leadership, a parent, or a Christian friend in whom you have confidence. They will pray with you, read Scripture with you, and help you to find the assurance that the Lord intends for you to have.

》 REMEMBER

For I am not ashamed of the gospel
of Christ, for it is the power of God to
salvation for everyone who believes, for
the Jew first and also for the Greek.

—Romans 1:16

kidnapped
by angels
Acts 12

》 PURPOSE

When Peter was imprisoned for preaching the gospel, not just prayer but *constant prayer* was offered on his behalf. We see in Acts 12 that believers were earnestly praying, but didn't actually believe their prayers had been answered when Peter showed up at the door, free from prison. God wants us to pray expecting Him to answer, and to be ready when He does.

》 BACKSTORY

The imprisoned Peter was about to be executed, but he slept so deeply that the angel sent to free him had to shake him awake. Peter followed the angel, thinking he might be dreaming as he watched gates open on their own to let them pass. When the angel left and Peter realized that what was happening was real, he went to the house of his friends—a house where prayer meetings were a regular thing and the people could be trusted. At

A.D. 33	A.D. 33-59	A.D. 60-61
Birthday of first church	Acts of apostles	Book of Acts written

this time, the church that had begun with a few new converts had now grown to over eight thousand, and it continued multiplying throughout the world to bring the good news.

» CHARACTERS

Herod Agrippa 1: A Jew by birth, grandson of Herod the Great, he did not follow the law. He died shortly after Peter's escape from prison. Because he blasphemed God, Herod was struck by an angel, eaten by worms, and died while still wearing his royal apparel (Acts 12:21–24).

Peter: The disciple who denied Jesus three times but went on to live a life of service for Christ and later died for Him; author of 1 and 2 Peter.

John Mark: A cousin of Barnabas, the man known as the Encourager. He traveled with Barnabas and Paul as their assistant, or minister in training.

Rhoda: A servant girl at the church in Jerusalem.

Angel: A heavenly messenger sent by God in the form of a human man for the purpose of guiding and protecting Peter.

» THINK: PUT YOURSELF IN THE STORY!

Herod the king, who persecuted the church, killed James the brother of John with the sword. When Herod saw that the Jews were happy about this, he put Peter in jail also, with a squad of soldiers to guard him, with the intention of giving the people more of what they wanted. He would wait until Passover was finished, when he would have the Jews' full attention, and make a big show of executing Peter.

The church offered constant prayer to God for Peter, who was bound in chains between soldiers with guards at the door. While he was asleep, an angel came to Peter, poked him in the side, and said, "Get up quickly and put on your sandals and your clothes." Peter was amazed and thought he might be seeing a vision, but even so, as the chains fell off his hands Peter did as he was asked and followed the angel out. Together they passed undetected by two guard posts, through the iron gate to the city—which opened for them on its own—and down a street before the angel departed.

EMERGE | N | ENGAGE

> No guards, no gates can keep God's work undone.

Peter came to himself and thought, *This must be real!* So he went to the house of Mary, the mother of John Mark, where many were gathered in prayer. He knocked at the door; a girl named Rhoda came to answer, but when she recognized his voice, she was so excited that she left him standing there while she went and announced to the prayer group that Peter was at the gate. The group told Rhoda she was crazy or that maybe it was an angel, but she kept insisting.

Peter kept knocking until they opened the door. Seeing Peter, the group was astonished, and Peter motioned to them to be silent as he came in and told the story of how the Lord brought him out of prison.

The next day Herod searched for Peter and had the soldiers put to death who had guarded him. Shortly after, an angel struck Herod with death because he blasphemed God, *but the word of God grew and multiplied* (Acts 12:24).

》 DREAM: JUST IMAGINE IF . . .

> **When there is much prayer, there is much power. When there is little prayer, there is little power; and when there is no prayer, there is no power.**
>
> Charles Spurgeon

EMERGE|N|ENGAGE

Read Acts 12:5. Our primary tool in effective ministry is constant prayer. How can anyone pray *constantly*?

1. Literally, praying for someone means *thinking*, or spending quiet time in mind and heart, on behalf of a person before the throne of God; praising God in prayer is *thinking* about Him, our love for Him, our gratitude, the wonder of who He is.

   Constant prayer means that we do not depend solely on evening or morning prayers or on prayer times with others, but we add to these prayer thoughts throughout the day, as we go. We develop a habit of praying *constantly*.

What is the biggest hindrance to *constant prayer* in your life? (Hint: Quiet! We can't seem to find any. Music, texts, tweets, conversations, TV, movies, and friends are just a few examples.)

So when could you carve out a little *quiet* time? Go for a walk; hide in your room without anything digital or electronic; turn off the phone.

2. Read Acts 12:5 and compare it to Acts 12:24. How are these verses related?

pray: to think about earnestly in worship; to intercede on behalf of a person; a specific request to God

All power comes through prayer. When we pray, we are trusting God to draw people to Himself. The early Christians knew this, and we see that their prayers were not about their own problems; rather, they prayed for boldness and power so they would not fail in proclaiming Christ. God answered their prayers by allowing them to speak the gospel with boldness so that none could stand against them.

3. We must understand the power to change lives is not ours. It doesn't matter how polished our presentation of the gospel is, how authentic our lifestyle is, or how much knowledge we have about the Bible. The power to boldly proclaim Christ and see lives changed comes from the Spirit of God, who opens people's hearts to hear the message of Christ (John 6:44). We have the privilege of being co-workers with God in building His kingdom. Our job in this process is to pray for non-Christians and to be obedient to the Spirit when He opens doors to share our faith. In regard to non-Christians, pray that:

» God will draw them to Himself (John 6:44).

» They will seek to know God (Deuteronomy 4:29).

» They will believe the Scriptures (1 Thessalonians 2:13).

» Satan is bound from blinding them to the truth (Matthew 13:19).

» The Holy Spirit will work in them (John 16:8–13).

» God will send people to share the gospel (Matthew 9:37, 38).

» They will believe Christ is the Savior (John 1:12).

» They will turn from their sin (Acts 17:30, 31).

》 They will confess Christ as Lord (Romans 10:9, 10).

》 They will surrender all to follow Him (Philippians 3:7, 8).

(Adapted from the Impact Bible)

Who is on your heart that needs Jesus as Savior? Write his or her name here and then select three verses above you can use to pray and "think about" their salvation.

I am praying for: _____ to come to know Christ as Savior.

FLIPSIDE

What might have happened if this group of Christians (who prayed on behalf of Paul) just gave up and stopped praying?

4. Look at Acts 12:14–15. Remember, God hears your prayers. It's kind of funny that Peter's friends prayed so earnestly for him yet didn't even believe it when their prayers were answered and Peter showed up right at their door. They even told Rhoda she was crazy!

The answers to our prayers may not always be as dramatic or immediate as Peter's encounter. God's answers to our prayers range from "No" to "Go":

No = What you are asking for does not align with His will for your life.

Slow = What you are asking for is right but it is not yet time.

Grow = What you are asking for is right but you are not yet ready to receive it.

Glow = When you do not know what to do, do what you know to do.

Go = Everything fits together; God is giving you the green light!

Which answer(s) to prayer are you experiencing in your prayer life right now? Why do you think that may be the case?

》 LEAD: EARN THE RIGHT

1. So far we have looked at miracles in the lives of Luke, Peter, Paul, and Stephen as well as in the amazing, explosive growth of the early church.

EMERGE|N|ENGAGE

What have been the key characteristics so far in these lives that have allowed God to use them as spiritual leaders? Which characteristics have caused the Lord to hold back?

Luke 24:25 _____

_____

Acts 4:13 _____

_____

Acts 6:3 _____

_____

Acts 6:8 _____

_____

Acts 9:10 _____

_____

Acts 12:5 _____

_____

DO-OVER

Based on the verses in the Emerge |N| Engage section, what are two characteristics you would like to "do over" in your life?

_____

_____

2. Matthew 4:18–20 says, *Jesus, walking by the Sea of Galilee, saw two brothers, Simon called Peter, and Andrew his brother, casting a net into the sea; for they were fishermen. Then He said to them, "Follow Me, and I will make you fishers of men." They immediately left their nets and followed Him.*

Have you ever thought about your purpose? What is it God is calling you to do?

purpose:
the reason for which something is created; for which something exists

List five roles in your life (for example, student, brother, daughter, Christian):

1.

2.

3.

4.

5.

Now, beside each role you listed, write one task or project you can work on this week that pertains to each of those roles. You will then have a week lived of *purpose!*

EMERGE|N|ENGAGE

They were fishermen by trade, but Christ called them to a higher purpose, and they immediately followed. One was about making a living (fishing); the other was about a purpose or life mission.

3. James died for Christ; Peter was ready to. You will probably not be called upon to die for His name, but it is something to think about. Would you die for the cause of Christ? Before you answer, ask yourself, "Am I *living* for the cause of Christ?" The answers to these two questions are dependent on one another.

You can read in John 15:18–25 that Jesus warned His disciples of persecution to come. When you read this, do you understand that it is not *you* who people reject but *Christ?*

4. Below, read Philippians 1:21 in three different Bible translations:

》 To live is Christ, and to die is gain (NKJV).

》 For my life is about the Anointed *and Him alone.* And my death, *when that comes,* will mean great gain for me (The Voice).

》 To me the only important thing about living is Christ, and dying would be profit for me (NCV).

Write Philippians 1:21 in your own words. What does that verse mean to you? Write at least five sentences if you can and really think about what it means to *live in Christ, for Christ, a life about Christ alone.* Explain your thoughts as best you can, perhaps using an illustration or example from your own life.

》 REMEMBER

> *"Therefore I say to you, whatever things you ask when you pray, believe that you receive them, and you will have them."*
>
> —Mark 11:24–25

they turned the world upside down
Acts 17

》 PURPOSE

In these days of constant change, life is anything but predictable, and in Acts 17, Paul modeled a flexibility we can learn from as he faced stress and surprise in three different cities. When he saw an opportunity to spread God's Word, he took it, rolling with every interruption and disappointment. A good leader prepares and plans to reach goals, but must be prepared for difficult situations and stay consistent even when things don't go as planned. The ability to be flexible makes the journey about gaining insight and wisdom along the way rather than just arriving at a destination. (Adapted from the Impact Bible)

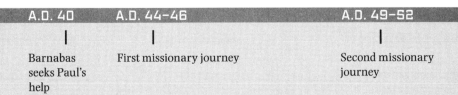

A.D. 40	A.D. 44-46	A.D. 49-52
Barnabas seeks Paul's help	First missionary journey	Second missionary journey

》 BACKSTORY

This is the second of four missionary journeys undertaken by the apostle Paul. In this chapter he visited three cities, all of varying sizes and cultures, yet his modus operandi remained the same. He connected and communicated as he engaged the crowds in debate and discussion of Christ. In each city Paul faced persecution and imprisonment but unashamedly and boldly proclaimed the Scriptures, trusting the Holy Spirit for the results.

Thessalonica was on the "super highway" of that time called the Egnatian Way, built for the military purpose of moving legions quickly from one part of their empire to another. It was a major seaport, the capital of Macedonia, and a strategic Roman military station with a population of some two hundred thousand. It is often said that when Paul preached in a city, it either saw revival or rebellion; in this city it was both. Paul had to escape again, this time to Athens. The Greeks in Athens were seekers, open to new ideas and thought, and spent a great deal of their days discussing philosophy. Athens was a university city, known for culture, education, and idolatry; in fact, some wrote there were more idols there than people. Paul took advantage of the seeking mentality, learned about the idols, and studied the culture in great detail. (Adapted from the Impact Bible)

》 CHARACTERS

Luke: The author of the Book of Acts; a physician and a co-worker with Paul.

Paul: The apostle persecuted for his preaching of the Word, he was focused and faithful to the finish.

Silas: A prominent member of the Jerusalem church, he traveled with and for Paul to various New Testament churches, dedicating his life to the furtherance of the gospel.

Timothy: Paul's fellow traveler and a servant to the churches. He was a young man, and Paul told him, *"Let no one despise your youth, but be an example to the believers in word, in conduct, in love, in spirit, in faith, in purity"* (1 Timothy 4:12).

Stoics: A group of Greek philosophers who believed everything was God, and man's life was a small spark of that spirit and was returned at death. They believed everything that happened was the will of God and should be accepted without resentment.

Epicureans: A group of Greek philosophers who believed everything happened by chance; death was the end and the gods were aloof to the cares of man, remote and distant from the world.

》 THINK: PUT YOURSELF IN THE STORY!

Thessalonica

Paul's custom throughout his ministry was to go to the synagogue of the Jews, and he spent three Sabbaths in the synagogue in Thessalonica reasoning from the Scriptures, explaining and demonstrating that Christ had to suffer and rise again from the dead, and saying, *"This Jesus whom I preach to you is the Christ"* (Acts 17:3). Some people believed, a great many of them devout Greeks, and many leading women of the city joined him and Silas in their work.

Some of the Jews became jealous of Paul's popularity and brought evil men whose convictions were for sale, gathered them into a mob, and set the crowd into a frenzy to attack the house of Jason, a prominent man and devout Christian, where they thought Paul might be. The mob shouted to send out those *who have turned the world upside down* (Acts 17:6).

Berea

synagogue:
the building where a Jewish assembly or congregation meets for religious worship and instruction, no matter how large or small the city

Paul's buddies sent him and Silas away under the cover of darkness to save his life, even though it was a dangerous time to travel. As soon as Paul arrived in the small town of Berea, he went right to the synagogue again and found the people there open to searching the Scriptures. Many believed, including the Greeks, both prominent men and women.

When the Jews who had caused trouble in Thessalonica heard about this, they came and stirred up the crowds to anger again. So once again, Paul's friends planned an escape, this time by sea, and brought him to Athens while Silas and Timothy stayed behind in Berea.

Athens

When he saw pagan gods and idols across the city of Athens, Paul immediately went to the synagogue and began talking with the Jews and then with the Gentile worshipers in the marketplace. He faced people of all kinds of religious thought there, including Stoics and Epicureans.

Some called Paul a *babbler* and others said he taught of foreign gods and a strange resurrection (Acts 17:18). Those who wanted to know more took him to Mars Hill, the site of an Athens government council where new ideas were often presented. They asked him what this new doctrine was that he talked about, saying, "We want to know what these things mean" (v. 19).

Paul boldly stood right in the middle of the platform and addressed the many pagan idols and altars. He said, *"I perceive that in all things you are very religious; for as I was passing through and considering the objects of your worship, I even found an altar with this inscription: TO THE UNKNOWN GOD*" (Acts 17:22, 23). Paul wanted them to know that God could be known! He told them, "God made the world and everything in it, since He is Lord of heaven and earth, does not dwell in temples made with hands, and He needs nothing from us, but it is He who gives life, breath, and all things to all mankind . . . He is not far from any of us; for in Him we live and move and have our being. He now commands all men everywhere to repent, because He has appointed a day on which He will judge the world; He has given assurance of this by raising Jesus from the dead."

Now when the people heard what Paul said about the Resurrection, some mocked, but others wanted to hear more. Paul left there and went to Corinth, but a few in Athens believed.

EMERGE:

- Paul's motivation was from above.

- He was not superman; he had to emerge from the habits of the past and take on a new life.

- Goal setters prepare and plan, allowing for interruptions, disappointment, and difficult people. This is called *flexibility*.

ENGAGE:

- Paul's habit was to go to the synagogue, a place of worship, to find people who might be open to discussing the Scriptures. In every city he visited, he took the offensive position by presenting the gospel first, not waiting to see if he would be well received.

- He also went to the marketplace, where he knew there would be many types of people.

- He communicated and had discussions with people rather than just "telling" them.

- He was aware of the dangers, but did not take these into account.

A turn involves two things: a *terminus a quo* and a *terminus ad quem*. It involves turning *from* something and a turning *towards* something."

William Barclay

» DREAM: JUST IMAGINE IF . . .

1. Look at Acts 17:2. It says Paul went into the synagogues *as his custom was*. We might say it was his habit. If someone were to describe your habits and the places you go to hang out, what would they say?

More importantly, what are your intentions and motivations when you do go to hang out?

repent: turn from sin; turn to God

Paul was motivated to tell people of salvation; just as he had received.

FLIPSIDE

What values do you reflect through your online sites and communication? What do your postings say about you to unbelievers, friends, and family?

What kind of influence do you think you are having on others by the way you communicate through text, Twitter, and posting?

2. Paul demonstrated "the spirit of nevertheless." He went to the synagogue three weeks in a row before there was a single convert. Can you think of a time when you might have given up too soon on unanswered prayer or on a person you were trying to influence? Is there someone in your life right now that you are thinking of giving up on?

In Acts 17:5 we see some believed, but some criticized and caused conflict. Success will always be accompanied by opposition. It happened to Paul; it will happen to us. Paul knew this going in because there was a time when he had been the one doing the criticizing!

Read Acts 7:57–58 and 8:1–3. (Remember, Saul is Paul's name before his conversion.) These verses show us a man (Saul) who was angry and difficult, persecuting Christians for no reason other than intolerance. His encounter with the living Christ took him from the shadows of anger and emerged him into the world as a proclaimer of the truth.

3. Notice that everywhere followers of Christ went they taught and spoke of the *resurrection* of Jesus Christ:

》 If you confess with your mouth the Lord Jesus and believe in your heart that God has raised Him from the dead, you will be saved (Romans 10:9).

》 Jesus Christ our Lord . . . declared to be the Son of God with power according to the Spirit of holiness, by the resurrection from the dead (Romans 1:3, 4).

》 Then He said to them, "Thus it is written, and thus it was necessary for the Christ to suffer and to rise from the dead the third day, and that repentance and remission of sins should be preached in His name to all nations" (Luke 24:46, 47).

What is the big deal? Why is this one doctrine—the belief that Jesus was resurrected from the dead—so important?

4. There were a lot of voices shouting at Paul, mostly those of jealousy, anger, and hatred. But he heard another voice above the crowd; it was the voice of God.

Think about the white noise in your life—shouts of the crowd, blaring of the media and music, and digital messages. With that constant racket, is it even possible to hear the voice of God?

List two ways to make a new habit of hearing the voice of God:

1. _____

_____

2. _____

_____

» LEAD: EARN THE RIGHT

1. Acts 17:2–3 says that Paul *reasoned with them from the Scriptures, explaining and demonstrating that the Christ had to suffer and rise again from the dead, and saying, "This Jesus whom I preach to you is the Christ."* Remember that Paul had only the Old Testament to work with. How would you *explain and demonstrate* that Christ had to suffer and that He rose from the dead?

2. Paul was run out of the famous city of Thessalonica and sent to Berea, a city of under twenty thousand. Human emotion might have been the lead dog here if Paul had allowed it to be. He could have become depressed, felt unappreciated, and even given up. But he didn't. His first response was faithfulness.

Do you sometimes want to give up? Have you ever been discouraged over not being chosen for a team, position, or to be part of a certain group of friends? Have you become depressed about constant temptation because staying strong on your own was too hard? What motivated Paul? How did he keep focused and inspired? (Refer back to Acts 9.)

What do you think will help you to stay focused and faithful?

Notice that Paul always traveled with companions, co-laborers, and people who were of the same mind and heart—prayer partners who stayed on track in their goal to keep him accountable and strong. List two people you can count on to "travel" with you through the temptations of life.

List one person you know you need to stop hanging out with if you are to stand strong:

DISCUSS

Leadership is not just a title or position; it is not just getting others to follow. Leaders take the time to equip and empower others so that they too can lead.

DISCUSS

The measure of success is determined by faithfulness to the truth, regardless of circumstance.

> > > >

3. Paul and Silas were defined as those who *turned the world upside down* (Acts 17:6). But sometimes we as Christians look more like those who blend in. What specific influence can Christians have on our culture to turn it *upside down?*

How can individuals have specific influence? Through dress, language, habits? Give specific examples.

How about a church youth group? What can they do in word, actions, or example to have influence on the world?

4. In Acts 17:16, when Paul arrived at Athens, he was alone. As he waited for Silas and Timothy to arrive, he saw great opportunity and was moved to begin boldly proclaiming Christ. Leaders sometimes have to go it alone; they take initiative.

FLIPSIDE

Do you think things might have gone differently if Paul just hung out, blended in with the crowd, and waited for Silas and Timothy to arrive? Why or why not?

"Opportunities are seldom perfect. but when one is flexible. as Paul was. they can be doors that lead to a greater privilege and a resulting testimony of strength. courage. and faith for generations to come."
Jay Strack

5. Great influencers are first great connectors. They care about people, listen to their viewpoints, and earn the right to be heard.

Paul appealed to the curiosity of the people he preached to and he knew their culture. One thing that made him so effective was that he could debate their beliefs. He went about the city studying the statues and learning about the idols and philosophers the people trusted in.

Review Acts 17:22–31 to see how Paul talked with the people about their culture. Notice in verse 28 that he even quoted a popular poet in order to bridge communication: *for in Him we live and move and have our being, as also some of your own poets have said, "For we are also His offspring."*

》 REMEMBER

But as many as received Him, to them He
gave the right to become children of God,

to those who believe in His name.

—John 1:12

emerge
and engage
Acts 26

》 PURPOSE

In Acts 9:15 the Lord Jesus said, *"[Paul] is a chosen vessel of Mine to bear My name before Gentiles, kings, and the children of Israel."* When the time came, Paul handled this call well, without pageantry or celebrity. In Acts 26, as Paul is brought to testify before government officials, he shows how opportunity and motive go hand in hand.

》 BACKSTORY

The apostle Paul used a phrase time and again throughout his ministry: *obedience to the faith.* In Acts 26 he wanted the governor and king and all of their courts to know that he was a man faithful to the message of God. This is the biblical definition of success. We see nowhere in the account that Paul was intimidated by the celebrity of the officials or the royal guards to whom he presented his personal story of salvation, although

A.D. 33	A.D. 33–59	A.D. 60–61
Birthday of first church	Acts of apostles	Book of Acts written

it would have been easy to have been intimidated. Pageantry was every-where in the royal courts, and these men held in their hands the power to save or destroy Paul's life.

It is important to know that at the time Paul stood before these officials, he had already been bound in prison for two years under the previous governor, Felix (see Acts 24:25–27). Felix heard Paul speak and was afraid of the judgment Paul proclaimed, but wanted the favor of the Jews, so he just left him in prison. When Festus replaced Felix as governor, it was rumored that Paul still had the relief offerings taken for the church at Jerusalem, so Festus called Paul often to come and have conversations, hoping he might use some of the money as a bribe.

Paul could have bought his way out of prison by asking his brethren for bribe money, but *obedience to the faith* defined his life. As a result, the Lord used Paul's imprisonment to give him access to powerful men in the government, giving him the chance to tell the story of salvation even to kings. (Adapted from the Impact Bible)

》 Many qualities can serve as a gauge for success, but only obedience to God can define it.

》 Obedience to the faith was the DNA of Paul's life.

》 CHARACTERS

Felix: The governor of Caesarea who imprisoned Paul.

Festus: He succeeded Felix as governor of Caesarea.

King Agrippa: The grandson of Herod the Great, the Roman appointed king of the Jews.

Bernice: The sister of King Agrippa.

Paul: The great apostle who was converted from self-righteousness to God's righteousness; a mighty proclaimer of the gospel to the Gentiles, the author of many New Testament books, a martyr for the faith.

》 THINK: PUT YOURSELF IN THE STORY!

As the Book of Acts progresses, it is easy to see that the chief priests and leaders of the Jews were becoming frightened of Paul because so many people were beginning to believe in Jesus. They brought serious complaints to the governor about him but had no proof of anything. The governor could not find a reason to punish Paul, so he asked King Agrippa to hear the charges in order to keep the Jews happy.

Paul came before Agrippa with respect, thanking him for the opportunity and acknowledging how informed the king was about Jewish customs. Then he began to tell his own story.

"I was a Pharisee myself, and now I am standing here because I say that God raises the dead. I do understand because I myself persecuted, imprisoned, and put to death Christians. But one day as I was doing this, I was on my way to Damascus and a light, brighter than the sun, shined around me and I fell to the ground. I heard a voice say in Hebrew, 'Saul, Saul, why are you persecuting Me?' So I asked, 'Who are You, Lord?' and He said, 'I am Jesus, whom you are persecuting. Get up for I have come to you for the purpose of making you a minister and witness for what you saw today and what I will show you. I will send you to the Jews and to the Gentiles to open their eyes to turn them from darkness to light and from Satan's power to God's that they may receive forgiveness of sins and the inheritance of eternal life by faith in Me.'"

"King Agrippa, I had to obey this heavenly vision from the Lord Jesus and started telling those in Damascus, Jerusalem, all of Judea, and then even the Gentiles, that they should repent, turn to God, and do good works. These are the reasons the Jews are trying to kill me. But understand I have only spoken of these things that the prophets and Moses said would come; that is, that Christ would suffer, that He would rise from the dead, and proclaim light to both Jew and Gentile."

Then Festus accused him of being crazy, but Paul replied, "No, I speak words of truth and reason. To the king I speak these things because he knows all about these Scriptures as they are open to all. King Agrippa, do you believe the prophets? I know that you do."

Then Agrippa said to Paul, *"You almost persuade me to become a Christian"* (Acts 26:28).

Paul replied, "I pray that you and all who are hearing me today might receive the Lord as I have."

After this the king, his sister Bernice, the governor, and those with them stood up and talked about what Paul had said. They could not find one reason to punish him.

》 DREAM: JUST IMAGINE IF . . .

1. Remember that this bold Paul the Apostle was once Saul the Persecutor: *As for Saul, he made havoc of the church, entering every house, and dragging off men and women, committing them to prison* (Acts 8:3).

   Here Paul admits his evil deeds: *I myself thought I must do many things contrary to the name of Jesus of Nazareth* (Acts 26:9). Talk about EMERGE! Paul has come from hating Christians and denying Christ to now risking his life to tell others about Him. His life's mission was to ENGAGE people of all social standings—from the poorest to the kings—about the message of personal salvation.

What about the people you stand before every day? What about them intimidates you and why?

2. The greatest possession of every believer is the story of his or her personal testimony of salvation. What keeps you from telling your personal story of salvation to those you meet?

Are you unsure you know how? Afraid? Concerned you will be laughed at?

3. Use the outline of Paul's testimony as he tells it to King Agrippa to write your own. Write one to two sentences about your life without Christ. For example, maybe you were fearful, didn't care, didn't understand, were confused, or couldn't make good decisions. Tell your story in *your* words. Paul wrote: *I lived a Pharisee. . . . I myself thought I must do many things contrary to the name of Jesus* (Acts 26:5, 9).

Write one to two sentences about how you knew that you needed Christ. For example, maybe you heard a Bible verse that moved your heart; someone prayed with you; you heard a song, a sermon, or a verse. Paul said, *"I saw a light from heaven, brighter than the sun. . . . I heard a voice. . . . And He said, 'I am Jesus'"* (Acts 26:13, 14, 15).

Write one to two sentences about how you received Christ. Did you pray, confess sin, invite Him into your heart? Did you accept His gift of eternal life? In your own words, tell about your own experience. Paul offered his will to the Lord in surrender, saying, *"Lord, what do You want me to do?"* (Acts 9:6).

Write one to two sentences about your life as a Christian. How is it different from your life before you became a Christian? Do you have the power and help of the Holy Spirit? Do you feel the peace, confidence, and assurance of eternity with Christ? Paul's faithful proclamation of the risen Christ was evidence to all who saw or heard of him of the changes Christ had made in his life.

Now, try putting together all the sentences you wrote and reading them to someone. There are no right or wrong answers; there is no best way to do it. It is *your* story and you can tell it just as you remember it.

》 LEAD: EARN THE RIGHT

1. One of the main points of the story in Acts 26 is that Felix, Festus, and even King Agrippa were *almost persuaded*. But, we know that *almost* isn't good enough.

   》 Festus was *almost* convinced, but did not want to lose favor with the Jews.

   》 Agrippa was *almost persuaded*, but his sister Bernice stood beside him, and she did not believe.

   》 Both Festus and Agrippa were concerned about losing their power and position if they believed, so they did not.

   》 But history reveals that they lost their power and position not long after.

   (Adapted from the Impact Bible)

Be careful what you hold on to if it keeps you from coming to Christ or living for Him. It will be gone one day anyway! Are you "all in" or "almost persuaded?" What is it that makes you an *almost* follower of Christ—friends, pride, habits, selfishness, just not paying attention to God's love for you?

2. Standing before some of the greatest powers of the land, Paul was not impressed, but he was respectful. He knew that God, not the men before him, sets up opportunity and takes it down. The Scriptures tell us that inner character is what gives leaders favor with God and man.

favor: acceptance, an attitude of approval or liking; support

> Let not mercy and truth forsake you: bind them around your neck. write them on the tablet of your heart. and so find favor and high esteem in the sight of God and man."
>
> [Proverbs 3:3, 4]

Favor—everyone wants it; everyone looks for it. Let's look more closely at the verses from Proverbs 3 in order to break it down:

mercy (*checed*—Hebrew): goodness, kindness, faithfulness

truth ('*emeth*—Hebrew): reliability, faithfulness, stability, consistency

write: to *engrave*, to create a deep mark that cannot be removed

heart: the inner man, mind, will, heart, understanding

Solomon, the author of the Book of Proverbs and the richest and wisest man alive at the time, was essentially saying, "Don't leave these behind, don't lose them; these are valuable!" These two qualities—mercy and truth—are to be worn around the neck; that is, they should be easily seen and apparent to all who meet us. They should be engraved on our hearts; that is, they should be a very real part of our inner character. Only then can we find favor with God and with man.

Compare a tattoo, which is an outward engraving, with a message engraved on the *heart*. What is the difference? (Hint: there are lots!)

 The doors of opportunity swing open on the tiny hinges of obedience."

Ike Reighard

3. Select one of the synonyms for mercy or truth in the definitions above and tell of a situation on any given day where you might display these (for example, in a friendship, with a teacher, to a stranger).

DO OVER

The purpose of guilt is to teach us how to repent of our sin and learn how to live a biblical life. Can you think of a time that you wish you had displayed mercy and truth instead of anger or lying?

Take a minute now to present this to the Lord for forgiveness and replay in your mind how you could have handled it differently.

4. Note that Paul had the chance to

» buy his way out of prison with Felix (Acts 24:26);

» talk his way out of prison with Festus (Acts 25:9, 10);

» and finally walked out of prison with Agrippa (Acts 26:31).

Through all of it, Paul's faithfulness to the message of Christ stayed true and strong. They kept waiting for something else; Paul let them know there was nothing else (Acts 26:32).

One has to wonder—when it comes to our own difficult situations, how often do we

» talk our way out (wasn't my fault; couldn't help it; blame game);

» buy our way out (do favors, make promises, accept bribes);

» give God the chance to walk us out?

5. Discuss the phrase "Commitment precedes achievement" as you read through Acts 26.

"Luke's account of the early church ends abruptly: one of the story's heroes, Paul, is under house arrest in Rome awaiting trial. Other sources will recount how Paul is later martyred in Rome, a victim of Nero's paranoia and cruelty.

"Luke's account has ended [at Acts 28] but the story about the acts of God through the church continues into our day. We are the characters in the current volume of salvation history. Through our faithful obedience, also empowered by the Spirit-wind of heaven, our stories are part of the anthology of God's new creation." (The Voice, page 1371)

» REMEMBER

Let not mercy and truth forsake you; bind them around your neck, write them on the tablet of your heart, and so find favor and high esteem in the sight of God and man.

—Proverbs 3:3, 4

LEADERSHIP BEGINS
AT THE **FEET OF JESUS**

SLU:101
STUDENT LEADERSHIP UNIVERSITY

EQUIP + ENABLE + EMPOWER = FUTURE LEADER

Visit us online at
STUDENTLEADERSHIP.NET
Or call
888-260-2900

For over 25 years, AtlantaFest has served the needs of the Church as being one of the longest running Christian Music Festivals in the nation. Over the years, AtlantaFest has ministered to hundreds of thousands of people, of all race, ethnicity, denomination and background. People travel from all across the Southeast each summer for an unforgettable worship experience. Our passion is to proclaim the Good News of Jesus Christ. Throughout the years, thousands have made commitments to Christ through the ministry of AtlantaFest!

www.atlantafest.com

ATLANTA FEST

STRENGTH·TO·STAND

STUDENT BIBLE CONFERENCES

The Strength to Stand Student Bible Conferences are designed to offer a well-balanced, intense conference that will challenge students to go beyond the surface of casual Christianity and foster them into a lifetime commitment to Jesus Christ. Born of a vision to see thousands of students congregating in the Great Smoky Mountains, these conferences are designed for students yearning for a deeper, more effective relationship with Christ. In addition to discipleship, students are given the opportunity to respond to the Gospel. Since 1987, the Strength to Stand Conferences have seen over 100,000 attendees and over 8,000 decisions for Christ.

Scott Dawson
Evangelistic Association